From Fighting To Thriving

*9 Relationship Hacks to create the relationship
you re seeking*

D1531587

Jess Garza

Dedication

For every couple striving to create a happy home. For all the husbands working tirelessly to understand their wives. For the women striving to fill the impossible role of the "perfect wife." But most of all, in honor of the relationship that has taught me these valuable lessons; my marriage.

Acknowledgment

I would not be where I am nor hold these valuable tools to share if it weren't for my role models, mentors, teachers, and above all, my husband. Lorenzo, you have been my rock, my hard place, and everything in-between. Our love affair has taught me so much about life, about love, and above all, about myself. Thank you for your patience and your willingness to set me free to be me. You truly are my ride or die, I love you.

My circle is tight, and to them, I am grateful for the accountability and feedback. Amy, your life inspires and intrigues me, and your wild spirit gives mine permission to set itself free. To Denise and Alex, your example has been one that I soak in deeply whenever possible. You are the living example I choose to follow and the mentors I cherish most when it comes to marriage and parenting. Right or Wrong...it just works, thank you for always being bold enough to speak your truth into my life. To Amanda, your eloquent way with words, your deep passion for learning, and your love for life are contagious, I am so amazed by you and grateful for our friendship. To Sarah, you are steady and constant in my sea of never-ending change. Thank you for your deep, thoughtful words, which always come at the exact time I need them. To both of my Lauras, thank you for being my mirror and for holding space for me to lose myself to find myself. Your friendships mean the world to me; my triple goddess gals.

About the Author

Who the heck is Jess Garza, and why should I read this book? I am not a psychologist or marriage specialist. I am twice married, once divorced...to the same man. Needless to say, my experiences have been unique when it comes to marriage.

In my quest to create a truly fruitful marriage (the second time around), I have studied relationships to find what works and what doesn't. Initially, this was simply an obsession in a quest to help my own relationship, but when I realized how many people struggle in this area, I felt a strong need for this information to be out there for other couples.

I have spent the past twenty years truly fascinated with marriage. You see, I jumped into my marriage very young, excited, and eager, only to be met with some pretty major disappointments. When my husband and I met, we fell fast and hard for each other and loved spending as much time together as we could, as most couples do. It felt a lot like the Princess movies I had watched as a young girl, like I had been swept off my feet by my one true love. My husband and I spent years, seven years to be exact, moving from madly, deeply in love to divorce. I couldn't understand how we got to that point. How did love like ours fall apart? How had we joined the divorce rate statistic? I loved him even after our divorce, and he loved me, so why was it so damned hard to be married?

This question sent me on a quest for knowledge. I sought out happily married couples and interviewed them to see what they had in common. What did they do that made all the difference?

Why were they happy while so many couples I knew were struggling and staying together for their children, or because dividing assets would be too hard or because it was familiar?

Throughout this time, my husband and I began a long journey of discovery. The road back to each other was one that required us to grow. When we re-married, we knew that we couldn't just pick up where we left off or return to business as usual. We had to take a new humble approach to actually getting to know each other. We had to find real examples of joyful, love-filled relationships that we could follow. We had to learn to listen for understanding and how to resolve conflicts without inflicting pain. It was a decade of expansion and growth for us— ten years of learning and growing together. After co-creating a marriage that I cherish, I have become even more intrigued by what it takes to have a happy marriage. To find out why some couples have so much fun and love between them, while others seem to loathe each other. I have attended seminars and spent countless hours reading books about marriage. It is my life's work to understand and share what I know about what it takes to create a joyful, happy relationship.

My hope is that my experiences, both good and bad, will benefit more than just me and my marriage. My hope is that this book will give couples tools that they can actually implement into their relationships. My aim is to assist couples in creating a relationship that feels like a warm blanket on a cold night. A place where each partner feels loved and understood. May this book's pages bless you and give you what you need, this is my soul's desire.

Preface

This is the book I wish I had found years ago when my marriage crumbled. This book is intended to be a roadmap for couples to follow. Its pages are filled with strategies that anyone can implement into their relationship at any point to create a more enjoyable experience of partnership. Marriage was intended to be a joyful place of refuge and synergy. These strategies have transformed my own marriage from one of turmoil into one filled with love, desire, collaboration, and admiration.

Contents

Chapter 1: Happy List

Marriage is a contract of lifetime togetherness, love, support, and happiness, but it might not always feel like the happiest place to be. Nowadays, it is downright difficult to make a marriage fruitful. Our fast-paced environments and increasingly complex lives can be quite taxing on a marriage. Partners are increasingly dependent on each other for their personal happiness. You often see an unequal distribution between the partners. One expects too much from the other in terms of financial, economic, intimate, and social needs,while the other might rely on their partner for all of the household chores, raising the children, and taking care of extended family. Honestly, both examples are simply too much of a burden on each of the two partners.

When it comes to couples with one source of income, the individual working outside of the home may feel that they are the only one with a real job. They may feel underappreciated, overworked, and neglected by their spouse. Similarly, the person at home taking care of everything may believe that their job is the most important one. They work all day chasing children, managing household tasks, coordinating family schedules, and wish they had more time for their spouse, and for themselves for that matter. They often feel under-appreciated, misunderstood, and emotionally drained. Then there are couples where both parties work outside of the home. They are both juggling careers, co-workers, bosses, and reaching for success, all the while trying to make time for each other. The household chores may be shared, but they both may feel like they're doing more than their fair share. Exhaustion invariably sets in, and their once happy marriage has turned into bickering, blame game they both wish they could escape.

In either case, it can be difficult to find the love that was once a place of refuge for both parties. They find themselves frustrated and exhausted. This frustration, if gone unchecked for too long, can be very detrimental.

Let's suppose a husband spends an entire day catching a deal at work, but it slips out of his hands. He comes home and flushes out the anger on his wife. No matter how he makes up for it, he already hurt the one person that was looking forward to seeing him all day. Or let's switch the situation, the wife had a busy day, and her husband comes home and is hit with her tantrums and complaints about how busy she has been and how she needs space from him. Such situations spoil the night for both of them, and it becomes a routine of avoiding each other over time.

Then again, some couples find themselves happy the majority of the time. Both partners respect each other and are kind and considerate of the eachother's feelings. They both recognize and appreciate what their partner does for them and are considerate of each other. They spend their time together in a happy state of mind rather than upset or bickering with each other. But the question is, how can two couples in similar routines live entirely different married lives? The secret lies in the *Happy List*. Stay with me, I'm going somewhere with this, I promise. As adults, we need to be mature enough to understand that happiness comes from within. You shouldn't depend on anyone else for your happiness, but rather, you must make yourself happy. When you come to your relationship as someone that is already happy, everything changes. Doing the things that bring you joy and make you happy will help to strengthen your relationship. When you are happy, you release your partner from the obligation of *making* you happy. That is not their responsibility...that is *your* responsibility. When you fall into a marriage routine, sometimes you forget this. You think that because you married the person you love, you should be happy; this simply is not the case. Being happy takes time and attention, just like anything else worth having in life.

I remember when I fell into the trap of believing that happiness comes from outside of myself. When I believed that if I made my husband happy, then I would finally be happy. I spent the majority of my time doing things that I thought would make him happy, all the while ignoring whether those things made me happy or not. I would cook things that I thought he would love and then be totally crushed if he didn't like it as much as *I thought he should.* I would clean the house spotless and wash all of the clothes thinking that he would see my hard work from the day and be blown away at my household skills and that him acknowledging would somehow make me happy. I was seeking happiness in so many ways, but none of them had anything to do with the things that actually bring me joy or happiness. I was looking outside of myself for happiness. Needless to say, this season of our marriage was wrought with hard feelings and resentments. Without realizing it and without intention, I was single-handedly destroying my happiness and, subsequently, my marriage with my co-dependent expectations and actions.

It is so important for each individual to find, or rather, re-discover what makes them happy. It could be something as simple as taking a walk or as big as painting a masterpiece. There is no right or wrong answer or social norm to adhere to. Each person will have specific things that make them happy, and that is a beautiful thing. Get clear on the things that really make you happy. This idea was first shared with me by my friend Amy, who also happens to be a life coach.

To prepare your happy list, do it by yourself. Start by thinking of a time when you were really happy, and then think about exactly what you were doing at that moment. Close your eyes and picture where you were, who you were with, what your surroundings were like, etc. Jot down a few different moments and remember them in detail. Do your best to truly feel happy as you walk back to these moments in time. Write down what you remembered, it's a great way to start your list. Repeat this activity until you have a few things to choose from. The more you do it, the easier it will become and the more variety you will have on your list.

As an example, a list might look like this:

MY HAPPY LIST

1. Walk my dog.
2. Drink a cup of tea.

3. Bake something.

4. Do a Project I find on Pinterest.

5. Go to the gym-sweat it out.

6. Read a book.

7. Journal my feelings.

8. Sketch out my feelings.

9. Cook fancy food.

10. Paint a wall.

11. Dance in my garden.

12. Prank someone.

13. Play music and sing along.

14. Take a hot bath

15. Get out in nature/take a hike.

16. Watch a RomCom or Comedy.

17. Do nothing... guilt-free.

18. Get a hot stone massage.

19. Make my favorite green drink/smoothie.

20. Go for a Spa day.

However "crazy" or "silly" your list may seem, embrace it. This list is only for you, it's not for anyone else. Discover and explore the things that bring you joy. As your life moves forward, your principles and needs will change. What works in one season of life might not work in another. Experiment with your happy list, add to it, try new things, and keep it simple! This list is a work in progress and a tool for you to actively use. It is not something to write once and toss aside.

Taking care of yourself is important and should be put before pleasing anyone else. It is the pathway to achieving self-fulfillment, resulting in high performance, not just at work but in personal life as well. Also, by doing so, you are not just doing a favor to yourself but to your spouse as well. When you are happy, you will show up in your relationship ready to give and to receive freely with no strings attached. The expectation for your spouse to make you happy will no longer be there, which frees you both from unrealistic expectations and the pain and arguments that ensue.

Everything else can wait, so don't compromise your happiness for anything! It is important to honor yourself and to find inner peace and joy. Your job can wait, and it should wait. You will flourish in your relationships and stay happier and healthier when you are taking care of yourself first. Learn to say 'No 'where it's due. Come from a place of desire, not of obligation. Be who you are, and live how you want to. Don't be a people-pleaser. Find opportunities in hard times and positives in negatives. Put your happiness first! When you are self-fulfilled and satisfied with yourself, you feel good about who you are and what you do. In this case, you feel happier and more content with your life and relationships. Use your happy list as a guide to your happiness; anytime you find yourself feeling unhappy, or falling into old habits of complaining or being confrontational with your spouse, get your happy list out and *do something* that is on the list. Take action, be proactive and true to yourself and make your happiness a priority in your life. Fill your needs internally, and then you will have the right mindset to interact with your spouse. Otherwise, you will always expect more from people and end up hurting your own expectations.

The happy list is not just for you, it's for your spouse too. Encourage your spouse to have their own list to pull from during their down days, after all, their happiness is up to them just the same way your happiness is up to you.

If you had a bad day, don't just come and flush it out on your spouse. Instead, ask for space; tell your spouse that you need to "fill your cup" first. Go through your happy list and find what you want to do to get back to normal, or at least ease out some of your frustration. Once you are done soothing your heart and mind, then you're ready to interact with your spouse. You will never go to bed disappointed with each other without a real reason if you consistently take accountability for your own happiness.

Chapter 2: Your 3 Things

A relationship works solely on the basis of mutual respect, care, and love. One who ignores the basic principles of a relationship is very likely to have only the worst of experiences within their relationships. Love is reciprocal, but not in the way you might currently believe.

First of all, let's begin with the definition of reciprocal. It is fundamental, and the relationship does not work without it. Reciprocity refers to the exchange of something for a benefit that is mutual. In the current context, it means that love, care, and trust are exchanged in an equal way to benefit both partners. This way, the relationship is equal. However, in order for a relationship to truly be reciprocal, each party must be giving from a place of no expectation. In a marriage, you don't give in order to get. You give because you are in Love. Period.

If a marriage is based on reciprocity in the normal sense of the word, you are simply giving because you expect something in return. When you are giving in order to receive something in return, you are trading. This is not love and inevitably ruins the relationship.

There is another level of complexity to this as well. At times partners are giving all that they can. They try to do whatever they can for the other person but somehow, there is still a lack. For example, in chapter one, I discussed a time when I was spending my time doing things that I thought would make my husband happy. I was not giving him what he perceived as love, I was giving him what I perceived as love. Yes, what one person considers love can vary quite significantly both individually and culturally. In order to show your partner love in a way that they will recognize it, you must first learn what that is. It all starts with communication and honesty. It begins with a conversation to better understand your loved one and with being vulnerable enough to share your true feelings about love.

In a relationship, you could say, love is the glue that binds everything together. When that glue starts to drip off, the partners slowly start to fall out, opening up the probability of an end to the relationship. Love is what makes life bearable. It is what keeps people going. The significance of love is beyond anything else in adult life. Humans are intrinsically in love with love! It is meant to be shared and given freely. So, let's show love to our partners in ways that they will recognize it. The whole point is that we truly want our loved ones to feel loved, right?

This chapter explores an effective strategy that you can apply to your life from day one of your relationship or day one thousand; it can (and should) be implemented at any time. You might even be surprised by how simple it is. Such sophisticated creatures, yet our need for love is solved so simply? It's funny to look back on my marriage and realize that just a few simple shifts have made a world of difference, and this is one of them.

My husband and I have been blessed by the people we are surrounded with. One such couple that we are lucky enough to call friends shared this strategy with us. They have been married for over thirty years, and the love between them is palpable and contagious! There are two parts to their strategy: giving and receiving but remember, we don't give in order to get.

When we are the giver, we are simply giving because we know it is how our partner receives love. When we both show up this way, magic happens!

Your 3 Things

The first aspect involves being the disperser and diffuser of love. If both partners focus on being givers, it will lead to a more equal and healthier relationship as one partner is less likely to feel exploited or alone. When you are both giving each day, there is no disparity. The second part requires that you become a receiver. Too often, we are so busy in life that the thoughtful actions of our loved ones go unnoticed. Take the time each day to truly receive the love from the actions of your partner. Recognize that they took time out of their day to do something so that you would feel love from them.

In order to give love in the best possible way, start with a conversation. Sit with your partner and ask them to give you three very specific actions that if you did them each and every day, he/she would feel loved. Then return the favor to your partner and give them three specific, easy to accomplish things that would make you feel loved each day.

Be open and honest with your partner. You do not need to shy away from what makes you feel loved. It is a beautiful thing to be able to bring love into your partner's life every day, so be sure that you give them the same opportunity. The three things should be simple enough that your partner can easily accomplish each day. Complication kills this strategy, so keep it simple. I am the type of person that learns from other people's examples. In honor of that, I will share our lists with you in hopes that perhaps it will make this process as simple as possible for you.

One of the three things for me personally is a love letter. I really feel loved when my husband leaves a short, concise, and loving note in the bathroom, near the mirror, in the car, or even a text on my phone. Anything from *"You looked great today"* and *"I love you so much"* to *"I can't think of a world without you"* and *"Looking forward to seeing you tonight"* works like a charm. It makes me feel loved and cared for, as well as fosters my love for him. It's truly beautiful and exciting to see the note sticking out from under the hairbrush or rolled on my handbag.

The second thing that makes me feel loved is physical touch and specifically sitting close to him. When we're on the couch watching TV or reading a book together, I really love it when my body is touching his. Sometimes when I forget to sit close to him, he pulls me in. This intimate cuddling time is something that makes me feel a lot better after a long and tiring day.

Thirdly, I really feel loved when he asks about my day. He listens attentively to everything I have to say, regardless of what it is. This is just such a heartwarming feeling as it helps unburden me from most of the problems, and just having someone who listens to me helps me to let go of the stress from the day. Often, when I am cooking dinner (which is how I decompress from the day), he will come in and offer to help, but really, he is there for the conversation. He pours me a drink and just listens as I talk about my day. It reminds me that although things will go up and down, he'll always be there listening to me.

Now, onto what makes him feel loved. He is absolutely fond of beans. Plain old, slow cooked pinto beans. I believe it is the nostalgic feeling of his mom making beans every morning when he was growing up, or maybe he just loves his bean and cheese tacos; whatever it is, I am happy to make them. He feels loved when he can reach into the refrigerator and heat himself something to eat, so I make sure there are always fresh beans waiting for him in there. The second thing that makes him feel loved is when I sit in his lap or right next to him. He loves for me to be near him, and there is no such thing as too close. The third thing he likes is for me to send him a picture during the day. Sometimes they are G-Rated and sometimes a little more risqué, he says they brighten his day and give him a mood and productivity boost.

I just want to point out that I am by no means and in no capacity generalizing here. There is a great deal of diversity in what makes you feel loved. For one, maybe just their partner opening the car door for them makes them feel loved, while for another, pouring the milk in their cereal is the love trigger. Humans are quite refined and specific in what they like, and everyone should be respected for their needs and desires.

Another thing to note is that there can be more than three things that make you feel loved. 'Three' is used in this tip in order to keep things simpler. Also, one should not shy away from telling their partner if one of the things that used to make them feel loved no longer does. Individuals adapt and change, and that's normal. Simply talk to your partner about it and replace that thing on your "three things list" with a new one.

This is a strategy that can help keep your marriage healthy and affectionate. It is not about adding three things to your never-ending to-do list. This is about getting to know your partner and what makes them feel loved and then being excited to have the opportunity to show them that love each and every day. The main thing you need to keep in mind is that it only works when there is effective communication. Both of you need to be comfortable, understanding and open with each other. Commit to each other that you will take responsibility and do your part. Commit to yourself that you want your partner to feel loved every day. If your partner misses a day, that does not give you permission to start a fight with them or be upset. It is simply an opportunity to show them grace and understanding. If you miss a day, give yourself that same grace. We are often most critical of ourselves.

Whatever things are on your partner's list, do them as best as possible each day. This strategy is meant to be done each and every day. I would recommend every married or soon-to-be married couple to incorporate this strategy in their lives. It's satisfying and enjoyable while being easy and simple.

Many people believe in giving grand gifts and expressing them through majestic gestures, which can be fun, and there is a place for that within a relationship. Still, sometimes you need to rewind and adhere to simpler ways to foster love and strengthen your friendship with your partner. Yes, I said friendship. Look at your partner as your best friend with whom you can share any secret, enjoy any experience, and treasure every day without the fear of being judged.

Marriage and everything related to it are truly splendid. Many people are unable to see that, but it's there. That splendor is always there. Love is a basic human need, and a marriage can be a place to foster that. By bringing love into your life through this technique or otherwise, you're doing what you were made to do as a human being; you're sharing and receiving love. So, go and get to it!

Chapter 3: Argument Crusher

The greatest, yet the least used tool a human has, is our mind and our ability to think. Like computer programs, we tend to do things the way we were taught and "programmed" to do them. Many people don't give enough thought to the way they think and where those thoughts originated from. We are all taught how to think by the people in close proximity to us that had the most influence over us and our wellbeing as children. Our parents, teachers, religious leaders, and role models all subject us to their way of thinking in one way or another. Many of us were taught that there is a right and a wrong way to do things. That if you aren't right, then you are wrong. We were taught to be right, but why? Why aren't we taught to be wise instead?

In our need to be right, we cut ourselves off from true connection. We take pride in being the one proven right, but we aren't taught to take pride in accepting the difference of perspectives. For children, this may work anyway, but once you grow up, it becomes a problem. We often argue over meaningless things and try to prove our points. We don't see that we're losing a meaningful relationship over it, little by little. As we all progress in life, we're often taught how to be right or fight for winning an argument. We are told that there is a right and wrong only, but we are never told that the best path lies in between the two. We try doing things that help prove our point somehow, but we miss out on what we lose in that process. This is something you can see throughout all relationships. So much time is spent trying to prove your point and that you are right in whatever discussion you're having, especially in a marriage. We don't realize it, but sometimes these arguments get to a point where you no longer listen to the other person for understanding. You listen only for responding and proving your point. So as your spouse is talking, you are not listening to what they're saying. You do not truly hear their needs. Instead, you are busy thinking about what you will say next in rebuttal to what they're saying. It's easy to come to this point within a marriage.

My husband and I found ourselves at this point too. We had been married for eighteen years and never realized that we were doing this. We were at a dinner event, and we started bickering back and forth over a useless topic. We didn't see that as an argument, it was just how we communicated with each other, but each of us was only trying to prove our points. We discussed how earlier in the day we had seen a friend, and we loved her new car. I expressed my love for the color of it. In my perspective, it was a bright red color.

My husband viewed that color from a different perspective. He said it was more of a burgundy color. So, we started trying to prove our points. I said it was bright, shiny, and gorgeous. He said it was such a deep red shade and that he had never really seen this color. We kept going back and forth, trying to prove our point to each other. A couple sitting across the table from us were people we had just met but are now lifetime friends. The gentleman interrupted our argument and said, "*Stop arguing about shit that doesn't matter.*" His words abruptly stopped us right in our tracks because we didn't feel like we were arguing at all. He said couples spend so much time "discussing" back and forth; they're arguing back and forth about stuff that does not matter. It can be about past occurrences; you can argue back and forth about how a particular chain of events unfolded in your past. Or it can be about something that you plan to do in the future, it can be about a passionate topic, and literally, anything can fan your flame; it can happen in any discussion.

He gave us a solution to this problem, a problem we didn't even know we had. There is an easy, simple way to end any discussion that seems to be going round and round without end. It can all end with a few simple words such as, "you might be right." So, when you find yourself going down a path of trying to prove yourself right while the topic doesn't matter, you can end that discussion just by saying, "you might be right."

Next, the gentleman sitting across the table from us asked us to try it, and he had my husband say those words to me about the red car. "*You might be right.*" Suddenly, there was nothing for me to argue about because he had already told me I might be right. There was no more rebuttal. There was no retort, and there was no response to give to him because he just gave me the win. Also, he didn't lose anything in the process. So, in communications with your partner, it can often become a matter of winning and losing an argument, but rather than trying to win or lose, wouldn't you just rather have a happy home? This argument Crusher, "you might be right," can take the heat off pointless and meaningless arguments. The key takeaway that I have here for you is to understand the power of your words. It is important to understand the difference between "you might be right" and "I have to be right." While one statement only strengthens a bond, the other contributes to building a gap in the relationship. Arguments can never be eliminated from a relationship, whatever kind it may be. However, what matters the most is the kind of argument that exists and how you respond to it. An argument that may require the opposing sides to become defensive is an unhealthy one and must be avoided or resolved quickly. One may have to compromise, but the strength it leaves in your relationship is worth the sacrifice. On the contrary, if the disagreement is communicated without criticism, contempt, or being defensive, it will help build your relationship. Such a disagreement should always be taken as a learning opportunity as it can positively impact both sides.

If you want to see your relationship at its best, learn to accept that you're not always going to see eye to eye with your partner, but handling it wisely is what matters the most. Take out time for talking over things, comprehend them without personal biases, and truly *listen* to what they are saying to you. Listen, not to respond, but to understand. Be prepared for compromises and make them wholeheartedly. Value your relationship over the meaningless arguments; it's worth it. If each of you can let go of the need to be right, then you'll have a much more cohesive and enjoyable marriage. Jot down these words and learn to say them whenever there is a need, *"you might be right."*

Chapter 4: Stay Open

Ever walked into a room and felt a change in your energy? Maybe your energy drops, or maybe you walk in and feel a sense of calm. We have all been there at some point in our lives, whether we realize it or not. We are all subject to other people's energy (moods).

For instance, one night, I was in an excellent mood. My day had been phenomenal, and I felt great! I was cooking dinner and enjoying a glass of sparkling water with lemon (my favorite drink). I was listening to my favorite music and dancing around the kitchen as I cooked. I heard the garage door open and felt excited that my husband was home. When the door opened, and he walked in, my energy level immediately dropped. I could feel that his energy was much lower than mine. He didn't even have to tell me about it; I already felt that his day was far from great. Maybe it was because of his body language or the look on his face, I could just feel that his day was not good.

When this happens, which it definitely will, one of you will have a bad day, trouble at work or traffic on the way home, or bad news from family, it's inevitable...it's real life! Instinctually what most people want to do is adjust their energy level according to their spouse's. That is natural human behavior. No one wants to make their spouse feel worse by being bouncy and bubbly while they are suffering. However, rather than dropping your energy, it would be in both of your best interests if you just try to stay open to your spouse about how their day went without letting their disposition affect yours. Your higher energy can impact their low energy in the same way that low energy affects high energy. Why not be the catalyst that turns their day around instead of them being the reason that your day heads downhill? Or, if they are the type that just needs a little space to decompress, then give them that. Tell them to go find their happy list and that you will see them for dinner later.

Talk to them, be welcoming, and listen to what they have to say. Try to put a positive spin on the negative things that happened to them or allow them some space if they're not looking for advice. If they need to talk about it, let them get it all out. Pretend that you are holding a large trash bag open and let all of their words fall into that bag. Let them "word vomit" into it for as long as they need. Make sure those words are going into the bag only. What they are saying likely just needs to be said so they can stop thinking about it. Remember, you are only offering them a trash bag; whatever they dump into it has nothing to do with you. Your job is just to hold the trash for them so that they can get rid of it. Then you close the bag and throw it away along with everything in it. This tool came to me from the amazing Allison Armstrong. Her strategies have radically changed the way I approach my relationships. I highly recommend looking her up.

When my husband walked through the door that day, I simply asked him if he needed me to "hold the trash bag for him." He said, "if you don't mind, I just really need to get this off my chest." It's amazing what even five minutes can do to cleanse your soul and clear your mind when you have had a rough chain of events throughout the day. After five minutes of holding the trash for him, we went on to have a great night together. Sometimes, you don't need someone to cheer you up or make you feel better. You don't want someone to lift up your mood or your energy. You don't want to talk about it. All you need is for someone to let you be the way you are. To give you the space to feel whatever you're feeling without judgment. On a different night, my husband walked in from another tough day, and I could see that he needed to be left alone. He didn't want me to try to make his energy better or lift his mood. He did not even want me to drop down my energy to meet his. He just needed to be left alone so that he could decompress from his day.

I appreciated what he wanted and respected it with sincerity. I went about my happy way of being and cooking dinner and gave him the space he needed. I let him go and do what he needed to do to fill his cup.

Oftentimes, we are put in situations at work that we carry home with us. Once we get home, we look forward to either flushing that situation down the toilet or lying in bed and escaping from it. For instance, when my husband came home, it would have been just as easy for me to close off and not want to be around him, ignore him, and push his energy away. I could have stayed in my happy zone and not cared about the fact that he didn't have a good day. Honestly, I didn't want him to ruin my good day; nobody would want that. Rather than making it *him versus me* situation, it was wiser and more loving to ask what he needed and to be supportive in that. Without holding any expectations of each other, stay open to the fact that we are all human. Each one of us is going to have rough days, great days, and everything in between. Give each other space and the allowance to be ourselves in difficult moments; instead of burdening each other with expectations. This will be constructive for your relationship.

As I was in a very good mood, enjoying every bit of the day, I could have expected him to join me and share my joy. I might even have tried to force that on him, but that was not where he was. Let's be honest, don't we all put expectations on our partners rather than meeting them right where they are? We do, although we shouldn't. Most of the time, when our expectations are not met, we end up in an argument which causes hard feelings, and over time ruins our relationship. Your relationship requires a lot of understanding from each side. At that moment, he could not just snap into being upbeat and dancing around the kitchen with me. He needed time to sort through his day, and then he could bring himself to a better mood to join me later.

We are all human, and each one of us has our individual journey while in the short time we are here. We might be sharing our lives as soul mates, but there is a lot going on outside of that too. Each one of us has our own path that we're on, and we need to get enough space to share the good and bad without the pressure of constantly trying to meet our partner's expectations. There should not be any expectation of what either of us should be like at any given time. We should be allowed to be who we are and express how we're feeling. It makes for a lot less strife in the relationship.

Conclusively, I want to stress the importance of space. Let

your partner live and not just survive. You want them to live a life of their own, grow, adapt, and evolve. You want them to know that you'll be there for them when they fall. Note that forcing someone to fit into a preset mold is the worst thing you can do to your partner.

Throughout our lives, we are forced to conform to certain norms and values or certain molds set by society. The school, family, workplace, and every other aspect of human life in society ask that you fit into a mold. Don't make your relationship yet another overburdening and exhausting mold for your partner to fit into. Let them be who they are and meet them right where they are. It is very likely that you and your partner are very different. Those differences are probably what attracted you to them in the first place. Let them be who they are, and keep your heart open to them.

When people don't act the way we want them to or they do things that we disagree with, we often close our hearts to them. We close off and protect ourselves from pain by not being open with our partners. This doesn't serve you or your partner. A healthy relationship is not built upon or forced upon actions and suppression of feelings. It builds on love, trust, and openness. If you can allow space for your partner and stay open in your relationship, that's the best favor you can do for yourself, your partner, and your relationship.

Chapter 5: Stay Conscious

In Chapter 3, I mentioned how we are all programmed as human beings during our formidable years. Throughout these years, habits become rooted in us. These habits come from our teachers, family members, parents, religious leaders, and those with influence over us. As we move through our childhood, those habits become the unconscious behaviors of our adulthood.

If you've ever sat in your car to drive somewhere and twenty minutes later arrived at your destination without remembering how you got there, then you know exactly what I mean when I say "unconscious behaviors." When you sit in the car to drive, you don't consciously put your foot on the pedal. It is an action that you don't think about anymore, and yet it always happens the same way, like any well-known routine or habit. This is what I call the "auto-pilot" mode of living.

All those unconscious behaviors of putting the car in drive or putting your feet on the pedals are all just habits that our bodies and minds are very used to and can do without a lot of conscious thinking behind those actions. Another example might be doing the dishes. You can simply be thinking about your day, what happened, what your spouse said, what your kids said to you while you're still doing the dishes. Yet somehow, without thinking about it at all, the dishes get cleaned. Similarly, we do many things every day with little to no consciousness, especially when it comes to marriage.

Once the honeymoon phase of marriage ends, we begin to

create habits within our relationship. A toilet seat is left up, and that triggers annoyance. She is only half listening when he mentions a work function they need to be at, and on the day, she forgets all about it and is rushing to get ready on time which triggers annoyance. You get my point; throughout the years, each partner creates their own set of unconscious behaviors and reactions within the relationship.

If you spend some time considering the unconscious behaviors within your relationship, you will likely find that you go unconscious more than you realize. For starters, let's say that when someone speaks to you in a specific tone, your unconscious learned behavior responds in the same tone without even thinking about it. You try to match their style, and often you can easily find yourself in an argument with your partner without consciously being aware of how you got there. Does that sound relatable? Think of a time that you found yourself in an argument. Has it ever felt like you are arguing just for the sake of arguing? Like, there is nothing really at the root of it, yet somehow the argument just keeps going? These are learned behaviors. Unconscious ways that we show up in our relationship. One person sounds argumentative, so their partner matches their tone, and the next thing you know, you're in a heated debate over...nothing.

If you unconsciously respond every time, you will quickly continue down the rabbit hole of unconscious responses, which is a scary place to be in within a relationship. To truly enjoy your relationship, it is important that you stay conscious more often. 'Bringing consciousness' to it means the exact opposite of being on autopilot at any given time. You need to be very conscious and aware of your actions and reactions. Think back to my driving the car example; the moment you thought to yourself, "wow, I don't remember a single moment of the drive," that is the moment you are conscious. Those are the moments you want to bring into your relationship. You are in the present moment, not thinking about yesterday or tomorrow or what needs to be done, you are truly present with your loved one.

When your spouse is talking to you, you may begin to feel that your mind and body want to respond in a specific, familiar way (unconsciously). At that moment, when your consciousness is aware and ready to control your response, instead of responding the way you always would, you get to choose your response based on how you really feel rather than a learned set of behaviors or habits. Imagine the effect this can have on your everyday experience of your relationship.

You can also be conscious in the way that you show love to your partner every day because you're purposeful in your actions when you're present-minded. When you are conscious and aware of what you're doing and not on autopilot, you will continuously bring better quality conversations and interactions with your partner at any given moment. It can be quite enjoyable to be present with the person you chose to share your life with. On the contrary, it can be painful when both are operating on autopilot. There was a time when my husband and I were unhappily married. We were both on autopilot for many years of our marriage. We were both cold to one another, and neither of us was present with each other most of the time.

Whenever something would arise, we would respond with the unconscious part of ourselves. I grew up in a family where you settle things by "who could scream louder or be meaner." I brought that with me to our marriage, I thought if I got louder than him and said meaner things, I would be on the winning side. Unconsciously, that's what I had been trained to do since childhood. My husband came from a family that when Mom got mad, Dad just drank it away. He was actually more fun when he was drinking.

I am sure you can imagine how bad these unconscious behaviors made our relationship over time. Whenever something arose that was uncomfortable, rather than being conscious and working through whatever the issue was, it just became a matter of, "okay, let me get louder and meaner," to win the conversation to which he would respond by pouring himself a drink and closing off. I was hurting my husband over the years without even realizing it. Not just that, but the more he drank, and the more I yelled, the less we connected. We became very distant from one another over time and let autopilot take over.

When he had finally had enough, he left. Being separated for a season gave me nowhere to turn except inward. I was forced to look at myself and at how I was showing up in the relationship. I was given a chance to look at who I had become. I realized I was not consciously aware of how I acted within my marriage until he was gone. There was no more getting louder than someone; I only had to deal with myself. Those emotions would still arise in situations, but I had to learn to deal with them more consciously because there was no one else to blame or yell at. The only thing I could control was myself. The only thing I could change was me. It was a dark period in our marriage, but it led to something beautiful, and for that, I am eternally grateful.

If things had continued to go the way they had been going, we would likely still be in a cycle of hurting each other. In taking a long hard look in the mirror and realizing how much I was unconscious in my relationship, I was able to change. I became conscious.

Through getting in touch with myself and acting in more conscious ways, I actually became more like the woman he fell in love with years before. I was me again. I was present with him and consciously made decisions about how I wanted to respond and who I wanted to be. I was no longer yelling in response to tense times, I was thinking about things before I spoke and was truly interested in resolutions when disagreements arose.

There was no longer a winner of any argument. Each disagreement became an opportunity to learn more about his needs, wants, and desires, and the same was true for him. We've spent the past eight years getting to know each other again and building what is now a beautiful relationship filled with love, trust, and conscious ways of showing love to one another. Our relationship is a forever-changing, always evolving adventure. In staying conscious with your partner, you get to bring a much richer experience to the relationship. It is no longer just trained patterns of ways of being. You get to choose your behavior. When you're conscious, you're deciding how you want to respond in each moment, and you're choosing how you want to show up. No longer on autopilot, you're able to create and build your relationship moment by moment, action by action, and thought by thought.

I have grown into a better person now. Whenever I feel that discomfort in my body is starting to arise, I ask myself questions internally before I respond. I understand now that old habits are still there, they don't just disappear when you decide to change, but I can recognize them now as they try to surface. It is a regular practice now for me to wait to respond. Whether it is my kids, my partner, or my employees, I don't respond until I have centered myself and gotten into the moment. So, when I am responding, I'm not thinking about what happened yesterday. I am not thinking about what might happen tomorrow. Instead, I am in the present while I deal with situations and respond in ways that are authentic to who I really am; not learned responses or habits.

When emotions start to arise, I question them instead of just giving in to them. I ask myself, is this how I feel right now? Or is this just "old stuff?" If it's just old stuff, I'm very swift to push it aside and say, "okay, well, how do I really feel right now at this moment"? This leads me to a much more conscious way of handling situations when they arise, regardless of it being personal or professional. Keeping yourself aware and conscious of what is happening in the present moment, rather than carrying forward feelings from your past, is very important for a healthy relationship. When you exchange vows with each other, it also means that you are opening a part of yourself to build with your partner. Every couple has a unique relationship that is in no way comparable to anyone else's. You must understand each other, build with each other, and stay conscious of what is happening in your relationship.

In preparation to write this book, I interviewed couples who have happily spent over 15 years in a marriage to understand what makes their marriage a happy one. I'm not saying that longevity is the only indicator of a happy marriage, not by a long shot. I have witnessed plenty of long unhappy marriages. I just know that a couple that has been able to weather the inevitable storms that life brings and stay together for at least that long and still be happy together have some tools in their marriage.

A common determinant of their content and healthy relationships was that they all tend to show up in a way that is not just how their parents showed up or the way they were programmed to show up. They are making conscious choices every day to love their spouse and act accordingly. They also said that they kept themselves very much aware of how they are treating their spouse each day. From my perspective, that is consciousness, staying attentive, and gaining insights every day within your relationship. This is quite the opposite of what you see in many failed marriages, where it is just two people operating unconsciously, and eventually, they can't do it anymore.

They think that it is a problem in the relationship, but really, it is all a matter of how they show up to the relationship each day that's causing the pain. If you want to have a relationship that is fulfilling and joyful, it starts with you. Show up in your relationship making conscious choices rather than a chain of unintentional, unconscious behaviors. Value your bond and create a happy forever by being purposeful and aware of the way you treat your partner. Stay in the present moment. You cannot change yesterday, and no one is promised tomorrow, so enjoy today together. That's the sweet spot in every marriage. Right here, right now.

Chapter 6: Anticipating What Is to Come

Marriage is not just a legal document or the act of sharing a house but is a bond of making a home together. It is a bond of deep, loving friendship and a promise of never-ending growth together. When you are in a marriage, you share your every reality with your significant other. You go through everything together as partners. Some days bring happiness and joy, while others bring sorrow and grief. What remains constant through all the ups and downs is the love and support you both give to and receive from each other.

The future is unknown, but the present can do wonders in shaping a better future. It was rightly said in the movie Forrest Gump, *"Life is like a box of chocolates. You never know what you're gonna get."* It is, therefore, better to anticipate what's next rather than to respond to circumstances as they arise. Being in "reaction mode" can add unnecessary stress and worry to a relationship.

A politician would anticipate what he will do if he gets elected, a businessman anticipates his future expansion plans, and even a chef anticipates the number of orders he will receive for a day. We plan for a grand wedding month ahead, we plan Christmas and New Year's parties weeks ahead, and we plan when we expand our families. If recognizing the future possibilities and planning for them is important in these areas of life, then why don't we anticipate and make at least a tentative plan for some inevitable, life-altering events?

Especially those things that could/would impact how we show up in our marriage. Some examples of such life-altering events could be; the loss of a parent, job loss, relocations for work, business opportunities changing, an increase in income, a decrease in income, natural disaster, etc.

An example in my own marriage was when my 22-year-old sister passed away. I was 16 years older than her; she was the baby of the family, and her death was sudden and very tragic for my entire family. It was a very tough time for me, and I was grateful to have my husband. He stood by me as I worked through the trauma and gave me the time and space I needed to heal and grieve. We never could have anticipated this specific loss, but we definitely had an over-arching understanding and agreement between us of what would be needed if either of us were to experience a loss in our family.

As much as we may deny and expect ourselves to know it all, you can't anticipate everything because accidents are going to happen, world events could transpire that you can't foresee, and there will always be some things that you can't anticipate. However, there are some things that are almost inevitable. You can do your best to prepare yourself and your partner for these known events of life. You and your spouse are likely going to experience the loss of a parent, or one of your pets might pass away; there are so many things that can be anticipated and planned for in life. My husband and I have spent the time to put together scenarios where if those things were to happen, we know what the other person's wishes will be. We already know how we need to support each other through different scenarios.

When you're in the midst of an emergency, or a tragedy, you're definitely not thinking clearly. You find yourself in a place of mourning and grief. At that moment, you cannot tell your spouse what you need them to do to help you get through it, or maybe you can't even think of it yourself. I'm not suggesting that it is healthy to expect bad things to happen. I'm simply suggesting that you take the time to truly understand what your partner will need and how you can best make it through tragedy together if it were to happen.

It is always better to think ahead and make necessary arrangements, this will most certainly ease the burden later. As said by Benjamin Franklin, *"By failing to prepare, you are preparing to fail."*

As an example, my husband and I have already come to an agreement that when either of our parents passes away, we will need time to just be alone; time to grieve. We have agreed willingly and, without question or complaint, pick up all of the slack around the house so that the loss can be processed without the added guilt. As we had already talked about this beforehand, when my sister passed away, there was no question that the agreement was inclusive of my sister. I found myself in a vulnerable state, and I couldn't see anything clearly.

I was able to grieve the loss of my sister without any kind of family burden on my shoulders, and I was allowed to be by myself as much as I needed or wanted. My husband took care of our children, the house, and everything else. He made sure everyone was eating, including me, and he never questioned *what* I was doing, he was only concerned with *how* I was doing.

The matter was already talked through, and he knew what I needed the most. He dropped everything and drove me to my family (18 hours away) for the funeral. He prepared everything without asking me for anything. He packed my clothes, packed for our children, and he ensured that our pets were taken care of in our absence, all without asking me for anything. Because of him, I got there on time, and he took care of everything so that I could just be with my feelings. Our anticipation of such future events was what worked wonders for me during this devastating event.

It is imperative, in my opinion, that as a couple, you sit down and talk about some of the things that *could* happen and put a plan together that supports each person in the relationship. Otherwise, the last thing you want when you're in the midst of trauma or emergency is to be trying to make a plan on the fly.

This recommendation came to us the year before my sister passed away. One of the couples that we love dearly told us about when one of them lost their mother. Their mother was only in her 50's when she passed away, so it was not anticipated in any way. With the help of counseling and other grief processes, they were able to process their grief without it having a negative impact on their marriage, but so often, events like this put such a strain on a marriage that significant problems arise. After the loss of their mother, they began to consider what other events in life could be anticipated and planned for. It made them think about and plan for possible future events, and they recommended that we do the same. Because of their advice, we had a plan in place in case either of us lost a loved one, and I am so grateful that we did. Death is not the only life-altering event that can be anticipated within a marriage. For example, when children leave the house, whether it be for college or to pursue their own life, it is a life-altering transition for the parents. Some of the things to consider in this situation are: How are you going to fill your time when the children leave? How will you adjust to having fewer people in your house that need you? Is there a specific hobby you will take up to fill in your newly found free time? Will you travel more? Will you get a pet to nurture? Asking these questions in advance and putting together a tentative plan with your partner will lessen the shock when the events unfold. The transition to being "empty nesters" can be a fun one rather than something that causes pain and disconnect within your marriage.

Understanding one another is very important for a marriage to be successful. However, everything cannot be understood, and every expectation cannot be met without making your needs very clear to your partner. Therefore, it is wise to have things anticipated and planned for prior to them taking place. Planning beforehand is better than reacting and regretting after the fact.

Chapter 7: Laughter

People say that laughter is the best medicine. I would agree and add that it is also one of the most important elements in your relationship. When a couple gets together, they share laughs that really draw them close to each other. They enjoy their time together and live in the moment with shared happiness and joy. They spend the day enjoying themselves, and before falling asleep, they often think back to what happened that day and share silent smiles.

Through the years, laughter can shift as your relationship progresses. You may start having children, getting promotions at work, and adding responsibilities as you evolve and "grow up." You start stressing over the expenses that come along with a growing family. There's a lot on your plate; buying a house, having to pay for a mortgage, financing vehicles, and bills to worry about. If you are not careful with all of this, the laughter can begin to fall by the wayside without you ever even noticing.

It might not happen intentionally. It's just that there's less to really laugh about because everything was new at the beginning of the relationship, and there wasn't much to stress over. It's amazing how much can change after just a few years. In the beginning, you're learning about each other, and the nuances of personality differences might make you laugh; everything is just so new and different, it is very easy to find reasons to laugh together. However, as time goes on, that can subside. The things that once made you laugh can become the things that irritate you over time.

Laughter might seem like a very small thing, but it is a huge aspect when it comes to relationships. Think about it, how often have you heard someone say, "He makes me laugh!" when talking about a new love? Laughter is a spark between two people, a connection point that brings joy. It helps you bond with your partner. In my opinion, laughter in a relationship is as important as love is. It may as well determine whether or not two people connect well with each other, couples love to laugh together.

Through my experiences, I have come across this opinion that it is sensible to make laughter a priority in your relationship. It lightens the mood and keeps both parties joyous. My husband personally has made it a priority to make sure that he makes me belly laugh every day. When he hears me laughing at some point during the day, he feels like he has succeeded at his job. He finds himself content when he feels that he has brought joy into my life, and my laughter is an indicator of a job well done.

While it may seem like marriage is all about love, rainbows, and roses, in reality, it isn't. There will be ups and downs, good days and bad days. What's important is that the laughter you share with your spouse does not fade away. Being able to laugh with your partner is a blessing that not everyone gets to experience. That intimate laugh between partners is different than laughing with a co-worker or a friend. It helps the two of you feel closer and more bonded with each other. My husband has to get creative with making me laugh sometimes. He does the best he can because he knows that laughter is so important to me and the relationship we share. He tells me that my laugh is contagious, and so when he makes me laugh, we end up laughing together. Even after 20 years of being with each other, we still manage to laugh together every single day.

I can recall a point in our marriage where it wasn't filled with laughter; we had actually stopped laughing. Everything was serious and focused on getting ahead and doing what we had to do every day. We were never fully in the moment and never made time to share our waves of laughter with each other. This went on for about five years. A part of me went missing during this period. The bond I shared with my husband was weakened day by day. I started getting frustrated, and the house suffocated me all the time. The spark was gone in our relationship, and so was the joy.

Life is always going to give you things to worry about. There will always be responsibilities to be handled as a couple or as individuals. Why let these things affect the happiness of our lives? It is important to make sure that these responsibilities don't take over your entire mind, and they don't steal your joy to the point where you are no longer laughing, specifically, no longer laughing together.

Laughing, chuckling, and reminiscing about funny events in your past with your spouse increases happiness —not just in your individual life, but in the life you and your spouse share. Laughter costs zero, and yet the gains are massive. Just hearing someone laughing can brighten your mood, especially when it is the person you love. Injecting a little humor into your relationship will always help it to grow and thrive. If you're not a person who finds humor attractive, or if humor doesn't come to you naturally, at least try to make up for it in any other way that suits the two of you. You could maybe watch a few stand-up comedies together, or see the bloopers of your favorite TV shows, or do anything that fills your lives with joy and brings a smile to your face.

My husband is naturally a very funny person, and I am pretty witty myself. For us, it doesn't take a ton of effort on our part to make each other laugh. The most effort we make is to realize and remind ourselves every day that we need this element in our lives. We try to be conscious of the fact that we can bring out that part of our personality each day to bring joy into the relationship.

Laughter is the most effective medicine and the most potent drug, as it quickly treats both the body and the mind. It is like a spa for your emotions. When you laugh, you are less defensive; you let go of your reservations and act more natural. When you become a part of a joke or tell a funny story, you are much more fun to be around. The energy you share when you laugh is contagious. Try not to laugh when someone next to you is belly laughing, it's near impossible.

Sharing a laugh does not only make us good at problem-solving when there's tension, but it can help a couple get closer, which in turn increases the attraction the partners have for each other. These random laughs are so much more important when your relationship starts to feel stale or stressed.

When you share a joke that only your significant other and

you understand, it can be a reminder of your closeness. With the passage of time, your inside joke can be shortened to just a word, a phrase, or a little gesture, the use of which will immediately give both of you a moment of love. These little things in a relationship can make a huge difference over time. It's the small things done well over a long period of time that make all the difference.

Find ways to integrate laughter into your marriage every day. It will drastically change the environment in which you live. It is not rocket science, but it is easily forgotten in a marriage that laughter is the best medicine.

*"And we should consider every day lost on which we have not danced at least once. And we should call every truth false which was not accompanied by at least one laugh." —**Friedrich Nietzsche***

Chapter 8: Catching Them in The Act

Imagine with me for a moment. Picture yourself as an employee at a Fortune 500 company. You are a top salesperson within the company. Your constant efforts have been generating good revenues for the company for months. However, your immediate supervisor never recognizes your efforts and only points out things that turn out unfavorable. For three weeks in a row, you surpass your sales quota and make the company hundreds of thousands of dollars without anyone noticing. Then, on week 4, you fumble and miss your quota by a small margin. Your boss calls you in and question you for missing your quota. You feel unappreciated, you feel like your boss doesn't recognize the things that you do.

You have been working more than your fair share for several years now, but your boss still gives you no recognition. On and on, it goes like this. Extra effort from you and no recognition from your boss. The CEO of the company appreciates your boss every time you make the efforts, not knowing that you even exist. The only time you hear from them is when they feel something's going wrong. Would you be able to stay at that job for long?

You're not going to stay in that job very long. Even if you do, you aren't going to put your wholehearted efforts into it. No one can stay that unhappy for very long, and marriage is no different. If all you point out are negatives in your marriage and make no efforts to appreciate the good side of it, your spouse is going to feel a lot like that employee. They won't want to stick around in that environment for very long. Even if they do, they'll be unhappy and dissatisfied with it, and their efforts in the relationship with show their dissatisfaction.

When you are in any relationship, and marriage is no exception to this, it is important to recognize and appreciate the good things that people do. People like to be acknowledged. It is a part of being human; we want other people to notice our efforts. When we're doing things right or doing things that make other people happy, it's very natural to expect appreciation in return. This is one of the basic needs of every person.

If you can be intentional about recognizing your partner's efforts, you can help them stay happy and motivated in the relationship. Not acknowledging the positive effort but pointing out problems is also a very natural thing, but it won't bring joy into your relationship. If you look for reasons to appreciate your partner, you will find a lot of them effortlessly.

For instance, if your spouse is doing something that makes you happy, proud, or makes you appreciate them, then acknowledge it and let them know about it. The more you can recognize those things; it inadvertently helps you appreciate them more for who they are.

We are inundated with negativity, there is no escaping that. Just turn on the news if you disagree with this statement. When we are surrounded by negativity, it becomes so easy to see the negative and to focus on negative things. Think about this; if someone you knew suspected that their spouse was cheating on them, they would be eager to catch them in the act of cheating to prove themselves right. My belief is, why not put that much focus into acknowledging your spouse for all of the things they are currently doing right? Then you may not ever have to suffer through having a cheating spouse. People that are happy in their marriage are much less likely to cheat. People that are constantly told what they're doing wrong could easily find refuge in the arms of someone else.

Catching them in the act isn't just a favor you're doing for your spouse. You're also helping yourself by acknowledging them and making them feel like you noticed that they'd done something good. They will feel motivated and make even more efforts to put a smile on your face. In return, you're also recognizing how much you appreciate and love your partner. You will eventually start to realize and appreciate who they are and how they show up for you. This will make you fall in love with your partner a little more every day.

I can look back at a very rough spot in my marriage where neither of us could find anything that we appreciated about each other. Every time we spoke to each other, it was only negative and all about what we disliked about the other. I was constantly nagging him about how much he worked and how little he paid attention to what was going on at home. The time I did spend thinking about him during the day was about the things I wish he was doing differently. We didn't have conversations; it was just an argument every time we opened our mouths. Days went on like this, then days became months; we became distant from one another.

Seeing my marriage at this dead-end was heartbreaking. No one ever anticipates a relationship getting to this point, and no one wishes to live in such a relationship, it happens over time. It happens by only seeing the bad or negative side of things. It happens by not appreciating what you have and who you fell in love with, to begin with. I didn't appreciate him for everything he was good at. I kept on highlighting the negativities, and his approach was no different. Instead of continuing down this negative path, I started writing in a notebook of simple index card-sized paper. Every night, I would purposefully find three things that I appreciated about my husband that day, and I would write them in this notebook. It felt hard at first, I had been so focused on the negative things that it was not easy to see anything good, so I picked easy things. I wrote things like, "I appreciate you for picking up our daughter," and "I appreciate you for putting your coffee cup in the sink."

As we were barely on speaking terms, I would take a picture of what I had written and send it to him via text. I kept following the same practice for months. Not only did it get easier to find things to appreciate, but it also brought me to tears as I began to realize just what an amazing man he is. I was brought to tears on many occasions as I focused on how much I appreciated him for who he was, not just for the things he was doing. Inadvertently, we were back to having conversations and getting along with each other too. We were no longer concentrating on what we previously saw as negatives in each other. We weren't focused on changing each other or wishing that we were different in some way, but rather we began to love each other for exactly who we are, rather than who we wished the other person was. We started recognizing and appreciating each other for our efforts in the relationship. It was no longer about having the "perfect partner" or changing each other into what we thought would make us happy. It was about appreciating each other day in and day out.

In any relationship, someone must take that first step. You can't stress over what your spouse does and does not do and let it ruin your relationship. You can't wait for your partner to be the one to change or to take the first step. Someone has to lead, why not let it be you if you're the one that's yearning for a better relationship and longing to have that sense of connection back with your spouse? Don't base it on what they're doing or not doing, do what you need to do to make it better. Take the first step, trust me, you will thank yourself later.

What I did in that notebook was one simple thing, and to this day, he still has it on his nightside table. I gave it to him as a gift for Christmas that year. On occasions, I've caught him just flipping through it to look at some of the things that I appreciated about him in that tough season in our marriage.

I started appreciating him more often, and his effort to make me happy and keep our relationship lively increased every day. It got easier for me to find things to cherish about our marriage because he was going out of his way to do things so that I would appreciate him and vice versa. It made me want to do things for him, too, so that he would appreciate me as well. It wasn't about being perfect or checking off boxes on a list. It truly became about loving each other and appreciating each other well. It became about showing up in a way that we appreciate each other no matter what. The good, the bad, and the ugly, and everything in between is recognized and acknowledged between us. It is something I can always fall back on during rough times. Finding three things that I truly appreciate about him on any given day can really lighten up my feelings for him, and when I acknowledge them, it does the same for him too.

Without getting too far off of my point of how important appreciation is, I want to acknowledge the fact that feedback will be necessary within a marriage. Inevitably, there will be room for improvement, a boundary that gets crossed, feedback needing to be given, or communications of what you would love for them to do that they aren't doing enough of or possibly not at all. It's important to keep in mind that more often than not, your spouse means you no harm. They actually just want to see you happy. So, in my marriage, when feedback is necessary, I always try to start with that in mind.

I start with a positive, and then the feedback ended with a positive. So, feedback might look something like this in my house: "Babe, I love you. I know you have been swamped at work. I'm hoping that we can spend a little bit more time together in the evenings. Could we do that? It always makes me feel so loved when we have time together in the evenings." In this example, there is no one pointing fingers or being accusatory, I'm not being a victim or trying to make him feel bad for working so much. I am simply asking for what I want in a loving way. While feedback will be necessary, when appreciation for what is right in your relationship is at the forefront, you won't have much to complain about.

Acknowledgment of effort and appreciation toward your partner are a few of the many keys to a healthy relationship. You can make your marriage fruitful by complimenting even the smallest of efforts made.

"Acknowledgement is the only way to keep love alive." –Barry Long

Chapter 9: Be a Safe Place

How many of us go through life trying to fit in? Whether it be into social constructs, parental expectations, workplace, and social norms...the list can be exhausting. Many people are taught from an early age to adjust who they are, how they act, and what they believe based on circumstances or other people's expectations of them. When you live a life of trying to fit in, it's so easy to forget how to be vulnerable because there simply is nowhere in your world that is safe enough to truly be you.

Do you have a place where you are free to truly express yourself? To just, be you? To like what you like and have the time and space to enjoy what you enjoy? I pray that your marriage is a place like this, if it's not, this may be the most important thing you read today. Your marriage should be one where you are truly free to be authentically yourself. A place that is safe and inviting for exactly that.

For far too many years, my marriage was anything but this. I spent the majority of my time thinking about the things that my husband would do that I didn't like; the things I wanted him to change about himself. We both walked on pins and needles, trying not to upset each other, taking score of the things we liked about each other and especially the things we didn't like. We pretended everything was ok and that it was normal to ignore the things we were feeling in order to try to save each other from the pain of having to talk about things that weren't working. You see, when you are pretending to like things that you don't, it simply means that you have expectations for people to meet in order to earn your love. Your love has conditions that must be met in order for you to give it; mine sure did. My husband and I became great at pretending and became completely numb to each other. True feelings could lead to pain, and pain could lead to an argument, and arguments led to more hard feelings, so it was just better to squash it all and feel nothing.

To just co-exist and live under the same roof. Raise our children together and build our business together but forget having any semblance of passion or true love between us. We loved each other because we said we would. We were married, and I thought marriage was like this for everyone. We had sex sometimes, it was part of the deal...you know, I said I would, and so I did. It was good *enough*, safe *enough* to just let things go unsaid and unaddressed.

The boiling point was when complaining to each other stopped altogether. We just stopped communicating about everything in order to avoid pain. He had his ways of numbing, and I had mine, and neither were unbearable to the other. It was a lonely time in our marriage. His way of numbing was with alcohol and my shopping and staying busier than ever so I wouldn't notice my loneliness as much. It worked great...until it didn't. Who wants to live in a passionless marriage? Not us, that's for sure, at least not forever! We knew what it felt like to be passionately in love, we had been there once, and we wanted it again. With a lot of work and continued practice of new habits (don't worry, I will share them later in the chapter), we were able to open the way for a new way of experiencing our marriage. When boiled down to the root of what was going on, it was so simple. Because of the way we approached each other, neither of us felt safe enough, to be honest; to be truly vulnerable with one another. We had created a marriage full of mistrust and fear.

If my husband was vulnerable enough to open up to me about something, he knew that in the very next argument, I was very likely going to use his very words against him. The same was true for him, if I was vulnerable with him about something I felt insecure about, he would tease me or bring it up later, which made me feel unsafe to share those feelings with him. We had slowly but surely built walls around our hearts in order to avoid the pain we had inflicted on each other over the years.

It has taken years of re-learning through repetition and commitment to create a safe place for each other. Our marriage was an amazing experience filled with passion and vulnerability. Somewhere we can both be honest with each other and feel free to be authentically ourselves, and it just keeps getting better!

As promised, it is my joy to share with you a few simple guidelines that may help you in creating your own safe place for you and your partner. Remember, these are just guidelines, I don't pretend to know exactly what your relationship needs are. Take what resonates with you and create the relationship that you've been seeking. Firstly, disagreements are nothing more than somewhere you go to learn something new. If you are in a disagreement with your spouse, it means you are about to learn something new about them that you may not have known before, so be sure to listen to the words coming out of their mouth! A disagreement just means that you don't agree. Thank God! Can you imagine if you agreed on everything all the time, that is like a ticking time bomb because if you agree on everything all of the time, one of you is not being honest! Be open to hearing what your partner likes and dislikes, what their preferences are. See if you can find a compromise and if not, it's ok to agree to disagree. Just remember, disagreements are nothing more than a conversation that should teach you something new about your partner, stay open and listen!

Secondly, everyone expresses their feelings and emotions differently. Some people cry, others may raise their voices, while some prefer to be alone to process things and gather their thoughts prior to having a discussion. The key is to remember that we are all different. Sorry to burst your bubble, but your way may not work at all for your partner. Give them the time and space to express their emotions in a way that is healthy for them.

Now, if your partner needs to yell to feel better, might I suggest that they get themselves a punching bag or take a ride alone to express those emotions prior to you having a conversation. The point I am trying to make is that we all need to be free to express our emotions and feelings without fear of judgment from the person we love the most. Create a way for you both to have this freedom. Nothing is worse for a relationship than emotions that are not expressed and end up bottled up and shoved down for years on end...at some point, that bottle will boil over, and it won't be pretty, I promise. It is such a gift to give each other; a safe place to truly express what you are feeling in a way that is healthy for you.

Lastly, embrace each other's differences whether it be the differences in your ways of expression or differences in your likes, dislikes, or sense of humor. Embrace the human that you chose to be with for WHO THEY ARE. We are all here on our own human journey, and each one is so different. How fun is it that you get to have a partner to share in your journey, and you share in theirs. We are not meant to change each other, we are meant to embrace each other in unconditional love and enjoy having a partner to do life with!

It really is that simple; let your partner be who they are and ask that they do the same for you. Embrace each other in love and have fun together on this journey called Life! Create your marriage to be the safest place for both of you. A place to be yourself and to never worry about what your partner thinks of you because you absolutely know that they love you unconditionally and you love them unconditionally.

Chapter 10: Conclusion

Marriage is not a thing of externality – not of family, religion, or finance – yet it is a string that holds two souls together. They mutually share a reality, one which only the two of them can see. It is not an obligation; instead, it is a deep and loving friendship, one in which there is love so strong that each would sacrifice their everything for the other. This sacred relationship is not limited to a legal contract; it is a beautiful, heartfelt bond that two people share. Some see it as a burdensome responsibility toward each other, but rather it deserves to be treated with the utmost care and respect. There is no other place that two individuals can come together to be as raw, real, and vulnerable with each other as you can within a marriage. Marriage is a place where a spirit can be truly free.

What they say is true; laughter is infectious. However, you know what? I think love is, too, not in the laughter kind of way, but in the constant, lifetime of commitment and devotion kind of way. To some people, love in a marriage might arrive slowly, while to others, it may be a clap of thunder kind, the kind that slaps you in the face and makes every hair on your body stand up. It may also be somewhat uncouth and shocking at times, but once you have felt the true feeling of love, you can never imagine a life without it. It won't always stay a thunderclap. Of course, there will be laundry to do and bills to pay – but under that everyday monotony, the love will still be there, alive and ever-growing. It will be warm, cozy, and just as real as it was the day the thunder clapped.

If you wish for your marriage to be fruitful, step up and work in that direction. Don't wait for your spouse to place the ladder for you to climb. You are responsible for the kind of relationship you make with your spouse, so start making it a heavenly experience or stop complaining about it. Complaining is just an easy way out for people that don't want to put in the work that it takes to be happy.

Making yourself happy is the first key to making your relationship a journey of joy. Prepare your happy list and take good care of yourself because you deserve it, and nobody else is responsible for doing that for you, not even your spouse. Don't expect your partner to make you happy. Rather, find yourself much more pleased when they do the unexpected things that do bring you joy. Putting unnecessary expectations on your spouse is one way to bring pain to both of you. Expect less and enjoy more.

Little things in life can make huge differences, and it is where the magic is. Look for the things about your spouse that make you feel good about them and the things that make you happy or proud to be their partner. Cherish those tiny things and appreciate them every day. Count the blessings in your life that you share with your partner and let go of the negatives as much as you can. Stay open to each other and pay conscious attention to your relationship. Disagreements are a very normal thing when it comes to relationships. Marriage is one of the deepest and most complex relationships you would ever experience. It won't be rainbows and butterflies all the time; there will be arguments and disagreements.

Listen to one another and pay attention to what is more important, winning the argument or building the relationship together! A disagreement is truly just an opportunity to understand more about your partner. It doesn't have to be an emotionally charged ordeal. Appreciate the little things your spouse does for you and let them know that you see it and praise it. Help them feel like a winner when they put a smile on your face or joy in your heart. The three very important things in this relationship are talking, talking, and talking. Talk to each other, know what your spouse expects from you in times they would need you the most. Listen to each other and understand each other the way no one else would.

People say that marriage means to develop a formal -legal bond between two people and their families. However, marriage to me is a never-ending promise of love, support, happiness, and togetherness. It is the thick and thin journey that you cross while holding hands and having each other's back. It turns a house into a home and individuals into a family. It is the purest of all relationships and requires your deepest feelings. If you understand and practice the ways to make a marriage successful, you can always build, improve or restore this bond with the right person, no matter what the age of your relationship might be. You will fall in love many times, but it can always be with the same person, and that's what marriage really is. As a very wise person once said, *"A husband and wife may disagree on many things, but they must absolutely agree on this: to never, ever give up on each other."*

FROM FIGHTING TO THRIVING

57